EMMANUEL JOSEPH

Evolving Empires, The Human Faces Behind Tech and Real Estate Success

First edition

This book was professionally typeset on Reedsy.
Find out more at reedsy.com

Contents

1

Chapter 1: The Foundations of Ambition

Every empire begins with a dream, and behind every dream is a
person willing to take the first step. In the worlds of technology
and real estate, the foundations of success are often laid in the most
unexpected places—a garage, a small office, or even a kitchen table. These
industries, though vastly different, share a common thread: the relentless
pursuit of innovation. The pioneers of these fields didn't just build businesses;
they built legacies that would shape the way we live, work, and connect.

Take, for instance, the story of a young programmer who spent sleepless
nights coding in a dimly lit room. Their vision wasn't just to create software
but to revolutionize how people interact with technology. Similarly, a real
estate mogul started by flipping a single property, driven by the belief that
spaces could be transformed into opportunities. These individuals didn't have
all the answers, but they had something far more powerful: an unshakable
belief in their ability to create something meaningful.

The early days were marked by trial and error, setbacks, and moments of
doubt. Yet, these challenges only fueled their determination. They learned to
adapt, to pivot when necessary, and to see failure not as an endpoint but as
a stepping stone. Their stories remind us that success is rarely linear; it's a
mosaic of perseverance, creativity, and resilience.

As we delve into their journeys, we'll uncover the human faces behind
these evolving empires—the fears they conquered, the risks they took, and

the sacrifices they made. These are not tales of overnight success but of unwavering commitment to a vision that transcended the ordinary.

2

Chapter 2: The Spark of Innovation

Innovation is often born out of necessity, a response to a problem that demands a solution. In the tech world, this spark has led to groundbreaking advancements—smartphones that connect us globally, algorithms that predict our needs, and platforms that redefine communication. Behind each of these innovations is a person who dared to think differently, to challenge the status quo, and to imagine a future that others couldn't see.

Consider the story of a tech entrepreneur who noticed a gap in the market for affordable, user-friendly devices. They didn't just create a product; they created an ecosystem that transformed how people interact with technology. Similarly, in real estate, innovation has taken the form of sustainable building practices, smart homes, and community-driven developments. These advancements didn't happen by accident; they were the result of visionary thinkers who saw potential where others saw limitations.

But innovation isn't just about creating something new; it's about improving what already exists. It's about listening to the needs of the people and finding ways to make their lives better. Whether it's a tech startup or a real estate project, the most successful ventures are those that prioritize the human experience. They understand that technology and spaces are not just tools or structures—they are extensions of our lives.

As we explore these stories, we'll see how innovation is not a solitary act but a collaborative effort. It's the result of diverse perspectives coming together, of teams working tirelessly to bring an idea to life. These are the moments that define an empire, the moments when creativity meets execution.

3

Chapter 3: Building Bridges, Not Walls

Success in tech and real estate isn't just about building products or properties; it's about building relationships. The most influential figures in these industries understand the power of connection—whether it's with customers, partners, or communities. They know that an empire is only as strong as the bridges it builds.

In tech, this means creating platforms that foster collaboration and communication. It's about designing tools that empower people to share ideas, solve problems, and create together. In real estate, it's about developing spaces that bring people together, that foster a sense of belonging and community. These leaders don't just see their work as a business; they see it as a way to make a lasting impact on society.

But building bridges isn't always easy. It requires empathy, patience, and a willingness to listen. It means putting the needs of others before your own and understanding that true success is measured not just in profits but in the lives you touch. These are the values that set the great apart from the good, the values that define a legacy.

As we journey through these stories, we'll see how these leaders navigated the complexities of human relationships. They didn't just build empires; they built trust, loyalty, and respect. These are the intangible assets that no amount of money can buy, the true markers of success.

4

Chapter 4: The Price of Progress

Behind every success story lies a series of sacrifices—late nights, missed opportunities, and moments of self-doubt. The road to building an empire is paved with challenges, and those who succeed are the ones who are willing to pay the price. They understand that progress comes at a cost, and they are prepared to make the necessary sacrifices.

In the tech world, this might mean investing years into a project with no guarantee of success. It's about taking risks, pushing boundaries, and sometimes failing spectacularly. In real estate, it's about navigating the complexities of the market, dealing with regulatory hurdles, and managing the expectations of stakeholders. These challenges test not just your skills but your character.

But the price of progress isn't just personal; it's also societal. As tech and real estate empires grow, they have a responsibility to consider their impact on the world. This means addressing issues like data privacy, environmental sustainability, and social equity. It's about finding a balance between growth and responsibility, between ambition and ethics.

As we reflect on these stories, we'll see how these leaders grappled with the weight of their decisions. They didn't just build empires; they carried the burden of their impact. These are the moments that define true leadership, the moments when you realize that success is not just about what you achieve but how you achieve it.

5

Chapter 5: The Power of Resilience

Resilience is the backbone of every empire. In the tech and real estate industries, setbacks are inevitable—market crashes, failed prototypes, and unforeseen challenges are part of the journey. What separates the successful from the rest is their ability to rise after every fall, to learn from their mistakes, and to keep moving forward.

One tech innovator faced countless rejections when pitching their groundbreaking idea. Investors doubted its feasibility, and competitors dismissed it as a passing trend. But instead of giving up, they refined their vision, sought feedback, and persisted. Years later, their product became a household name, transforming the way people interact with technology. Similarly, a real estate developer faced bankruptcy after a major project failed. Instead of walking away, they rebuilt their reputation, one small deal at a time, eventually becoming a leader in sustainable urban development.

Resilience isn't just about bouncing back; it's about growing stronger with each challenge. It's about maintaining focus on the long-term vision, even when the short-term seems bleak. These stories remind us that failure is not the opposite of success—it's a part of it.

As we explore these journeys, we'll see how resilience is not an innate trait but a skill that can be cultivated. It's about mindset, adaptability, and the willingness to embrace discomfort. These leaders didn't just survive; they thrived because they refused to let adversity define them.

6

Chapter 6: Collaboration and Community

No empire is built alone. Behind every tech giant and real estate mogul is a team of dedicated individuals who share the same vision. Collaboration is the lifeblood of innovation, and the most successful leaders know how to harness the power of collective effort.

In the tech world, collaboration often takes the form of cross-functional teams—engineers, designers, and marketers working together to create seamless user experiences. One founder recalls how their breakthrough came not from a single moment of genius but from countless brainstorming sessions, where diverse perspectives led to unexpected solutions. In real estate, collaboration extends beyond the boardroom to include architects, contractors, and community leaders. A developer shares how involving local residents in the planning process led to a project that not only met business goals but also enriched the community.

But collaboration isn't just about working together; it's about fostering a culture of trust and mutual respect. It's about recognizing that everyone has a role to play and that the best ideas often come from unexpected places. These leaders didn't just build teams; they built ecosystems where creativity and innovation could flourish.

As we delve into these stories, we'll see how collaboration transforms individual efforts into collective achievements. It's a reminder that success is not a solo endeavor but a shared journey.

7

Chapter 7: The Ethics of Ambition

A mbition drives progress, but it must be tempered by ethics. In the fast-paced worlds of tech and real estate, the pressure to succeed can sometimes overshadow the need to do what's right. The most respected leaders are those who prioritize integrity over profit, who understand that their actions have far-reaching consequences.

One tech CEO faced a critical decision when their platform began to compromise user privacy. Instead of prioritizing short-term gains, they chose to overhaul their systems, even though it meant delaying their product launch. Their commitment to ethical practices not only earned them customer loyalty but also set a new industry standard. Similarly, a real estate tycoon turned down a lucrative deal because it would have displaced a vulnerable community. Their decision to prioritize social responsibility over profit cemented their legacy as a leader who cared about more than just the bottom line.

Ethics in business is not just about avoiding wrongdoing; it's about actively doing good. It's about creating value that extends beyond financial returns, whether it's through sustainable practices, equitable opportunities, or transparent operations. These leaders prove that ambition and ethics are not mutually exclusive—they are two sides of the same coin.

As we reflect on these stories, we'll see how ethical leadership builds trust, fosters loyalty, and creates a lasting impact. It's a reminder that true success is measured not just by what you achieve but by how you achieve it.

8

Chapter 8: The Role of Mentorship

Behind every great leader is a mentor who guided them along the way. In the tech and real estate industries, mentorship plays a crucial role in shaping the next generation of innovators. It's about passing on knowledge, sharing experiences, and inspiring others to reach their full potential.

One tech entrepreneur credits their success to a mentor who believed in them when no one else did. This mentor not only provided guidance but also challenged them to think bigger and push harder. Similarly, a real estate developer recalls how a seasoned professional took them under their wing, teaching them the intricacies of the industry and instilling in them a sense of purpose.

But mentorship is not just about giving advice; it's about creating opportunities. It's about opening doors, making introductions, and providing a safety net for those who are just starting out. These leaders understand that their success is not just their own—it's a legacy that they have a responsibility to pass on.

As we explore these relationships, we'll see how mentorship creates a ripple effect, empowering individuals to achieve their dreams and, in turn, inspire others. It's a testament to the power of giving back and the enduring impact of shared wisdom.

Chapter 5: The Power of Resilience

Resilience is the backbone of every empire. In the tech and real estate industries, setbacks are inevitable—market crashes, failed prototypes, and unforeseen challenges are part of the journey. What separates the successful from the rest is their ability to rise after every fall, to learn from their mistakes, and to keep moving forward.

One tech innovator faced countless rejections when pitching their groundbreaking idea. Investors doubted its feasibility, and competitors dismissed it as a passing trend. But instead of giving up, they refined their vision, sought feedback, and persisted. Years later, their product became a household name, transforming the way people interact with technology. Similarly, a real estate developer faced bankruptcy after a major project failed. Instead of walking away, they rebuilt their reputation, one small deal at a time, eventually becoming a leader in sustainable urban development.

Resilience isn't just about bouncing back; it's about growing stronger with each challenge. It's about maintaining focus on the long-term vision, even when the short-term seems bleak. These stories remind us that failure is not the opposite of success—it's a part of it.

As we explore these journeys, we'll see how resilience is not an innate trait but a skill that can be cultivated. It's about mindset, adaptability, and the willingness to embrace discomfort. These leaders didn't just survive; they thrived because they refused to let adversity define them.

10

Chapter 6: Collaboration and Community

N o empire is built alone. Behind every tech giant and real estate mogul is a team of dedicated individuals who share the same vision. Collaboration is the lifeblood of innovation, and the most successful leaders know how to harness the power of collective effort.

In the tech world, collaboration often takes the form of cross-functional teams—engineers, designers, and marketers working together to create seamless user experiences. One founder recalls how their breakthrough came not from a single moment of genius but from countless brainstorming sessions, where diverse perspectives led to unexpected solutions. In real estate, collaboration extends beyond the boardroom to include architects, contractors, and community leaders. A developer shares how involving local residents in the planning process led to a project that not only met business goals but also enriched the community.

But collaboration isn't just about working together; it's about fostering a culture of trust and mutual respect. It's about recognizing that everyone has a role to play and that the best ideas often come from unexpected places. These leaders didn't just build teams; they built ecosystems where creativity and innovation could flourish.

As we delve into these stories, we'll see how collaboration transforms individual efforts into collective achievements. It's a reminder that success is not a solo endeavor but a shared journey.

Chapter 7: The Ethics of Ambition

A mbition drives progress, but it must be tempered by ethics. In the fast-paced worlds of tech and real estate, the pressure to succeed can sometimes overshadow the need to do what's right. The most respected leaders are those who prioritize integrity over profit, who understand that their actions have far-reaching consequences.

One tech CEO faced a critical decision when their platform began to compromise user privacy. Instead of prioritizing short-term gains, they chose to overhaul their systems, even though it meant delaying their product launch. Their commitment to ethical practices not only earned them customer loyalty but also set a new industry standard. Similarly, a real estate tycoon turned down a lucrative deal because it would have displaced a vulnerable community. Their decision to prioritize social responsibility over profit cemented their legacy as a leader who cared about more than just the bottom line.

Ethics in business is not just about avoiding wrongdoing; it's about actively doing good. It's about creating value that extends beyond financial returns, whether it's through sustainable practices, equitable opportunities, or transparent operations. These leaders prove that ambition and ethics are not mutually exclusive—they are two sides of the same coin.

As we reflect on these stories, we'll see how ethical leadership builds trust, fosters loyalty, and creates a lasting impact. It's a reminder that true success is measured not just by what you achieve but by how you achieve it.

Chapter 8: The Role of Mentorship

Behind every great leader is a mentor who guided them along the way. In the tech and real estate industries, mentorship plays a crucial role in shaping the next generation of innovators. It's about passing on knowledge, sharing experiences, and inspiring others to reach their full potential.

One tech entrepreneur credits their success to a mentor who believed in them when no one else did. This mentor not only provided guidance but also challenged them to think bigger and push harder. Similarly, a real estate developer recalls how a seasoned professional took them under their wing, teaching them the intricacies of the industry and instilling in them a sense of purpose.

But mentorship is not just about giving advice; it's about creating opportunities. It's about opening doors, making introductions, and providing a safety net for those who are just starting out. These leaders understand that their success is not just their own—it's a legacy that they have a responsibility to pass on.

As we explore these relationships, we'll see how mentorship creates a ripple effect, empowering individuals to achieve their dreams and, in turn, inspire others. It's a testament to the power of giving back and the enduring impact of shared wisdom.

[The book continues with four more chapters, delving into themes like adaptability, the intersection of tech and real estate, the importance of vision, and the legacy of evolving empires.]

continue

The server is busy. Please try again later.

4 / 4

continue

13

Chapter 9: Adaptability in a Changing World

The only constant in tech and real estate is change. Markets shift, technologies evolve, and consumer demands transform overnight. The leaders who thrive in these industries are those who embrace change, who see it not as a threat but as an opportunity to innovate and grow.

One tech visionary recalls how their company pivoted from a failing business model to a revolutionary platform by listening to user feedback and adapting to emerging trends. They didn't cling to their original idea; instead, they evolved with the times, ensuring their relevance in an ever-changing landscape. Similarly, a real estate developer shares how they shifted their focus from luxury properties to affordable housing during an economic downturn. This adaptability not only saved their business but also allowed them to make a meaningful impact on their community.

Adaptability requires humility—the willingness to admit when something isn't working and the courage to try something new. It's about staying curious, staying informed, and staying open to possibilities. These leaders didn't just survive change; they used it as a catalyst for growth.

As we explore these stories, we'll see how adaptability is not just a survival skill but a competitive advantage. It's a reminder that the ability to pivot is often the difference between stagnation and success.

14

Chapter 10: The Intersection of Tech and Real Estate

The worlds of technology and real estate are increasingly intertwined, creating new opportunities and challenges. From smart homes to virtual property tours, tech is reshaping how we buy, sell, and experience spaces. The leaders who understand this intersection are the ones driving the future of both industries.

One entrepreneur shares how they combined their expertise in tech and real estate to create a platform that simplifies property management for landlords and tenants alike. By leveraging data analytics and automation, they transformed a traditionally cumbersome process into a seamless experience. Similarly, a real estate developer partnered with tech companies to integrate smart technologies into their buildings, creating spaces that are not only functional but also future-ready.

But this intersection is not without its challenges. It requires a deep understanding of both industries, as well as the ability to navigate their unique complexities. These leaders didn't just see the potential of combining tech and real estate; they had the vision and expertise to make it a reality.

As we delve into these stories, we'll see how the fusion of tech and real estate is creating a new paradigm—one where innovation and spaces work hand in hand to enhance our lives.

Chapter 11: The Importance of Vision

Every empire begins with a vision—a clear, compelling idea of what could be. In the tech and real estate industries, vision is what separates the leaders from the followers. It's the ability to see beyond the present, to imagine a future that others can't yet envision.

One tech founder shares how their vision of a connected world drove them to create a platform that revolutionized communication. They didn't just see a product; they saw a way to bring people closer together, to bridge gaps and build relationships. Similarly, a real estate mogul envisioned a city where sustainability and community were at the heart of every development. Their projects didn't just provide housing; they created environments where people could thrive.

But vision alone is not enough. It must be paired with action, with the determination to turn ideas into reality. These leaders didn't just dream; they worked tirelessly to bring their visions to life, inspiring others to join them along the way.

As we reflect on these stories, we'll see how vision is the driving force behind every great empire. It's a reminder that the future belongs to those who dare to imagine it.

Chapter 12: The Legacy of Evolving Empires

The true measure of success is not just what you achieve but what you leave behind. In the tech and real estate industries, the most impactful leaders are those who build empires that endure, that continue to inspire and innovate long after they're gone.

One tech pioneer reflects on their journey, not in terms of profits or products, but in terms of the lives they've touched. Their platform has empowered millions, creating opportunities and connections that didn't exist before. Similarly, a real estate developer takes pride in the communities they've built—spaces that have become homes, neighborhoods that have become hubs of culture and connection.

Legacy is about more than just longevity; it's about purpose. It's about creating something that outlives you, that continues to make a difference in the world. These leaders didn't just build businesses; they built movements, leaving behind a blueprint for others to follow.

As we conclude these stories, we'll see how the legacy of evolving empires is not just in their achievements but in their impact. It's a reminder that the greatest success is the one that endures, the one that inspires future generations to dream, innovate, and build.

Book Description: *Evolving Empires: The Human Faces Behind Tech and*

Real Estate Success

In a world driven by innovation and ambition, *Evolving Empires* takes you behind the scenes of two of the most dynamic industries—technology and real estate—to uncover the human stories of resilience, vision, and triumph. This is not a book about faceless corporations or cold, hard numbers. It's about the people who dared to dream, who faced countless obstacles, and who built legacies that continue to shape our lives today.

Through 12 compelling chapters, you'll meet the pioneers who turned bold ideas into reality. From the tech visionary who coded their way to success in a cramped garage to the real estate mogul who transformed barren land into thriving communities, these stories are as diverse as they are inspiring. You'll witness their struggles, their breakthroughs, and the moments that defined their journeys.

But *Evolving Empires* is more than just a collection of success stories. It's a deep dive into the values that drive true leadership—resilience in the face of failure, collaboration in the pursuit of innovation, and ethics in the balance of ambition. It's about the mentors who guided them, the teams who supported them, and the communities they uplifted along the way.

This book is for anyone who has ever dreamed of building something meaningful. Whether you're an aspiring entrepreneur, a seasoned professional, or simply someone who loves a good story, *Evolving Empires* will remind you that behind every great achievement is a human being—flawed, determined, and endlessly capable of greatness.

Prepare to be inspired, challenged, and moved. Because the empires we admire didn't just evolve—they were built by people like you.

www.ingramcontent.com/pod-product-compliance
Lightning Source LLC
Chambersburg PA
CBHW061059050326
40690CB00012B/2677